Billy Marshall-S in 1947, and r several years w......g as a high school teacher, he spent four years at Papunya Aboriginal Settlement in the Northern Territory where he collected stories for use in a bilingual reading programme. Together with πO, Eric Beach and others, he helped found the Poets' Union of Australia. His first book of poetry, *Singing the Snake* (Angus & Robertson, 1990), has been hailed as a modern-day classic. Billy has also written for television (co-creator/writer of *Stringer*), and has made several documentary films. He is a graduate of the Australian Film, Television & Radio School, and a former member of the Playwrights' Studio (National Institute of Dramatic Art).

Order From:
Koala Books of Canada Ltd.
14327 - 95A Avenue
Edmonton T5N 0B6 Canada

ALSO BY
BILLY MARSHALL-STONEKING

POETRY
Singing the Snake — Poems from the Western Desert, 1979–1988.

SIXTEEN WORDS FOR WATER

A PLAY IN TWO ACTS

BILLY MARSHALL-STONEKING

Angus&Robertson
An imprint of HarperCollins*Publishers*

CollinsAngus&Robertson Publishers'
creative writing programme is
assisted by the Australia Council,
the federal government's arts
advisory and support organisation.

Sixteen Words for Water
was workshopped at the 1990
National Playwrights' Conference.

AN ANGUS & ROBERTSON BOOK
An imprint of HarperCollinsPublishers

First published in Australia in 1991 by
CollinsAngus&Robertson Publishers Pty Limited (ACN 009 913 517)
A division of HarperCollinsPublishers (Australia) Pty Limited
4 Eden Park, 31 Waterloo Road, North Ryde, NSW 2113, Australia

HarperCollinsPublishers (New Zealand) Limited
31 View Road, Glenfield, Auckland 10, New Zealand

HarperCollinsPublishers Limited
77-85 Fulham Palace Road, London W6 8JB, United Kingdom

Copyright © Billy Marshall-Stoneking 1991

This book is copyright.
Apart from any fair dealing for the purposes of private study,
research, criticism or review, as permitted under the Copyright
Act, no part may be reproduced by any process without written
permission. Inquiries should be addressed to the publishers.

Note: applications for permission to present this play by professional
and amateur companies must be made to the playwright's agent,
Almost Managing, PO Box 1034, Carlton, Victoria, 3053, Australia

National Library of Australia
Cataloguing-in-Publication data:

Marshall-Stoneking, Billy.
    Sixteen words for water.
    ISBN 0 207 17412 1.
    1. Pound, Ezra, 1885-1972 – Drama. I. Title.
A822.3

Cover drawing of Ezra Pound by Henri Gaudier-Brzeska
Cover design by Alison Windmill and Nicole Court

Printed in Australia by Griffin Press

5 4 3 2 1
95 94 93 92 91

THIS PLAY IS DEDICATED TO
EDWIN R. FIELD
TEACHER & FRIEND

Acknowledgements

Considerable thanks is due to Paul Thompson. He, more than anyone else, has lived through the process of the shaping of this play. His enthusiasm, sound advice and constructive criticisms have been invaluable.

Special thanks, as well, to Stefani Rigold and Maggie Gilson for their unflagging moral support; and to Edwin R. Field, Joe Stroud, Grant Caldwell, May-Brit Akerholt and Morton Marcus, who provided pertinent and useful criticisms of the work-in-progress. Also to Lynn Hard for his commitment and dedication to Australian poets and poetry.

I am also indebted to John Timlin, my agent; and to the Australian National Playwrights' Centre which selected an earlier draft of this play for presentation at the 1990 National Playwrights' Conference in Canberra. Also to Rhys McConnochie (who directed it), and to Simon Chilvers, Denise Kirby and Gia Carides (who gave an unforgettable public reading). I should also acknowledge the 1988 National Screenwriters' Conference in Queenscliff, Victoria, where — in reaction to comments made by Troy Kennedy Martin (re: micro-drama) — I first embarked on the play.

Finally, I would like to thank Wayne Harrison, Michael Lynch and the Sydney Theatre Company for producing the World Premiere production; and Tom Thompson, who saw fit to publish it.

And most of all — to Annie Marshall and Christopher Marshall for their love and light.

SIXTEEN WORDS FOR WATER

WAS FIRST PRODUCED BY
THE SYDNEY THEATRE COMPANY
AT THE WHARF THEATRE, SYDNEY, AUSTRALIA
ON 13 AUGUST, 1991,
WITH THE FOLLOWING CAST:

EZRA POUND	SIMON CHILVERS
WOMAN	ROSEMARY HARRIS
BETSY	MIRANDA OTTO

DIRECTOR:
RHYS McCONNOCHIE

DESIGNER:
KEN WILBY

DRAMATURG:
PAUL THOMPSON

Characters

Ezra Pound:
The poet, early 70s.

Woman:
A psychiatrist from the Department of Justice, Washington, D.C. Mid-30s

Betsy:
A university student. Early 20s.

The play is set entirely in Ezra Pound's room in Chestnut Ward, St Elizabeth's Hospital, Washington, D.C.

The year is 1958.

Note: The attention of actors and directors is called to *Ezra Pound Reading*, Vols. 1 and 2 (Caedmon Records, TC 1122 and TC 1155), which contain Pound's poetry as read by him. The present play was written with Pound's voice in mind.

Passages taken from Pound's work are signified by inverted commas, and should not be construed as indicating directions to actors.

INTRODUCTORY NOTE

In 1943, the American poet Ezra Pound was indicted by the United States government on the charge of treason. It had been alleged that Pound, an American citizen, had made anti-American broadcasts during the war over Italian radio and that these same broadcasts had given 'aid and comfort' to the enemy.

His wife, friends and colleagues, mindful of the war-born passions of the time and fearing for his life, urged him to enter a plea of insanity as a means of escaping the death penalty. This he did, and the plea was subsequently upheld by the court. Instead of releasing him, however, the government confined him to St Elizabeth's Hospital in Washington D.C., an institution which housed hundreds of the criminally insane. Pound — "one of the great literary figures of our time" — would remain incarcerated at St Elizabeth's for nearly thirteen years.

ACT ONE

BLACKOUT. Elvis Presley's HEARTBREAK HOTEL *emerges from the darkness.*

STAGE LIGHTS UP. MUSIC CONTINUES.

POUND'S *room at St Elizabeth's Hospital. Like the inside of a submarine. Wadded-up sheets of paper, trampled books, discarded newspapers, dirty clothes, battered cardboard boxes, old paint tins, dusty oil paintings, a couple of tennis rackets, etc. — the cargo hold on a Voyage to the Dead.*

Suspended over this chaos, running the length of the room, are several strands of twine to which are attached envelopes, charts and sheaves of manuscript: POUND'S *filing system.*

An old man, dwarfed by a larger-than-life wooden desk, hunches over an antique typewriter, asleep. His clothes are dishevelled; his hair, uncombed. He is EZRA POUND — The Poet.

A well-dressed WOMAN *in her mid-30s enters through the audience. She carries a briefcase. Her movements are clinical, precise, businesslike. She peruses the desk, scrutinises the filing system, and scans* POUND'S *unmade bed. She runs her index finger along the top of his dresser, checking for dust, then reaches over and switches off the radio.*

SILENCE.

POUND *stirs in his sleep.*

POUND: "They will come no more ... the old men ... with the beautiful manners."

The WOMAN opens her briefcase and takes out a notepad and pen.

POUND: "O god! . . . our god is a gallant foe that playeth behind the veil."

POUND emits a drawn-out moan, then raises his head. He runs his hands through his hair. His eyes dart over the topography of his desk as if searching for something he has misplaced. He sighs.

The WOMAN moves closer. Sensing her presence, POUND turns in his chair. Their eyes meet. POUND blinks, trying to dispel the apparition. He reaches out, tentatively, as if to test whether or not she is real. She pulls away.

POUND: A dream?

WOMAN: The Department of Justice.

POUND: Ah . . . a nightmare, then.

WOMAN: Doctor Overholser suggested the corridor, but I thought it might be more comfortable if we met in your room.

They both glance round the room.

POUND: Gives new meaning to the word "digs", wouldn't you say? What happened to the other one?

WOMAN: The other one?

POUND: The man. They usually send a man.

WOMAN: You mean Doctor Steiner.

POUND: That's the one. Gawd, how that man can talk! You couldn't get a word in edgewise.

WOMAN: From what I hear, you made quite an impression on him.

POUND: He liked the way I listened. We almost knew each other.

WOMAN: He used to talk about you a lot.

POUND: Always brought a bottle of whisky with him. The cheap stuff. Usually finished it, too. Why isn't he here?

WOMAN: I'm afraid Doctor Steiner won't be coming.

POUND: Not coming?

WOMAN: He's not with the Department any more.

POUND: Found another line of work, did he?

WOMAN: He retired.

POUND: Pity. He was doing such a good job, too. Lasted much longer than the others.

WOMAN: I'll be handling your case from now on.

POUND: (ASIDE) Must be the catalyst.

WOMAN: Pardon me?

POUND: Waal, I don't normally see people on Tuesdays. Busy schedule, you know.

WOMAN: Today is Friday, Mr Pound.

POUND: Friday! Well, there you have it! Three days lost already!

WOMAN: Doctor Overholser told you I was coming, didn't he?

POUND peers toward the audience.

POUND: Who else is here?

POUND stands and moves DOWNSTAGE.

POUND: You've brought someone with you.

WOMAN: No-one.

POUND: Shush! Listen!

The WOMAN follows his line of vision.

POUND: Sometimes I have the distinct impression I'm in a theatre. Everything's so goddamned unreal.

WOMAN: A theatre?

POUND: Yeah.

WOMAN: What sort of theatre?

POUND: Oh, I dunno. An ordinary theatre. An ordinary theatre with an ordinary audience. (WAVING) Hel-lo! Hello Doctor Overholser! I can see you!

POUND turns and moves toward the WOMAN.

POUND: Two-way mirror. Part of their therapy program. Can't scratch your ass any more without the feeling someone's watching.

WOMAN: You think Doctor Overholser is spying on you?

POUND: Of course he is. The man's a virtual peeping tom! Bloody unnerving. Everybody's so goddamned preoccupied with my private affairs. Voyeurism! It's all the go these days.

WOMAN: I'm quite sure Doctor Overholser respects your privacy.

POUND: Don't bullshit me! The man hangs on every word. The thought that he actually might miss something terrifies him.

WOMAN: He was telling me this morning that you seem quite contented here.

POUND: He would.

WOMAN: He was saying that you're one of his best patients.

POUND: Wish I could say the same for him.

WOMAN: I think he enjoys having you on the ward.

POUND: Oh yes. If he lost me his entire social life would evaporate. The man's voracious. Last week, he wanted to know everything I could tell him about Georgian poetry. Yesterday it was Byzantine art. And tomorrow . . . tomorrow . . . (REFERRING TO HIS DIARY) . . . ah yes, tomorrow he's pencilled in Confucius. Egad! There's no rest from him. I must be the only person on the planet the man can have a serious conversation with.

WOMAN: He probably thinks your ideas are worth listening to. You should be flattered.

POUND: Nobody who listens that closely can be trusted.

WOMAN: He seems to trust you.

POUND: He always knows where he can find me, that's why. He ain't like that by nature, believe you me. The other day he was convinced Bill Williams was trying to sneak in contraband. Can you imagine it?

WOMAN: Contraband?

POUND: So much depends
upon
a sharpened hacksaw,
glazed with cherries,
inside the homemade
fruitcake.
(PAUSE)
The man knows absolutely nothing about poets.

POUND opens a dresser drawer and takes out a bright red sweater with large, colourful geometrical shapes on it.

WOMAN: Thinks you're going to escape, does he?

POUND: Didn't you hear about Over-hauler's little wager? (BEAT) He's betting Barnes that Frost is going to spring me.

WOMAN: Doctor Barnes?

POUND: I believe he has five bucks riding on it.

WOMAN: I find that difficult to believe.

POUND: Five bucks, I know. A real gambler.

POUND slips on the sweater.

POUND: So . . . whaddaya reckon? A bit loud?

WOMAN: It's . . . it's very becoming. It's you.

POUND: A spinster in Schnectady, New York, made it for me. Knitted it herself. Blind since birth . . . took her three and a half years. A real fan.

POUND picks lint from the sweater. He looks up.

POUND: What're you staring at?

WOMAN: Was I staring?

POUND: I don't care what you call it; you were looking at me.

WOMAN: I'm sorry. It's just that, well . . . I would've taken you to be a much bigger man.

POUND: Everybody's a critic! Actually, I am not as short as I look. It's just that the ceilings are a mite high.

POUND gathers up a stack of newspapers from a chair and drops them on to the floor.

POUND: Take a seat, my dear. Make yourself at mental home.

WOMAN: Thank you.

The WOMAN crosses to the chair. POUND chucks another stack of newspapers from his desk on to the floor.

POUND: Ignore the mess. It's always like this.

The WOMAN sits as POUND tidies his desk.

WOMAN: I'd like to ask you some questions.

POUND picks up a plate of leftover pate. He sniffs it.

POUND: Dammit! I thought pate lasted forever.

POUND chucks the plate and pate into a wastepaper basket, and continues tidying up.

WOMAN: Mr Pound?

Continuing to tidy up.

WOMAN: Mr Pound.

POUND: What?

WOMAN: I was hoping we might have a little chat . . . you know, about some of your ideas.

POUND: I loathe chats.

WOMAN: Please. Don't think of me as the enemy. I assure you, that's not my role.

POUND: Now I'm worried.

WOMAN: I can imagine what you must be feeling.

POUND: I don't think so. But what about you? What're *you* feeling? (MOVING CLOSER) Yes . . . it's all over your face.

WOMAN: It is?

POUND: Don't be so coy. Look in the mirror! Go on! There's no use trying to hide it. You can't hide it!

WOMAN: Hide what?

POUND: It's all right. I can take it.

WOMAN: I'm not hiding anything, Mr Pound.

POUND: Doesn't bother me in the slightest.

WOMAN: What are you talking about?

POUND: You think I'm paranoid, don't you?

WOMAN: Paranoid?

POUND: See! Just rolls off the tongue, doesn't it?

WOMAN: A little sensitive, maybe, but . . .

POUND: You bet I'm sensitive! I've watched em.

WOMAN: Who?

POUND: The people in charge here. The clipboard brigade. The way they huddle together. They think I don't know, but I do. I know all about em.

WOMAN: Mr Pound, why do you suppose you are here at St Elizabeth's?

POUND: They didn't tell you!? (IN UTTER DISGUST) Bureaucrats!

WOMAN: I'd like to know what you think.

POUND: Well . . . that certainly puts you in the minority. (BEAT) Have you read my poems?

WOMAN: No. No, I haven't.

POUND: Essays?

WOMAN: Not yet.

POUND: What about my *Guide to Kulchur*?

WOMAN: No.

POUND: Not a scrap?

WOMAN: Nothing.

POUND: Well, how could you possibly be interested in what I think, then?

WOMAN: I'm interested in what you have to say.

POUND: What about the translations? (BEAT) Or the play?

WOMAN: I diagrammed sentences in high school and studied science and math at college.

POUND: Well, what do you read?

WOMAN: *Science Weekly*, *The New England Medical Journal*, *New Psychology*, *American Medicine*, *Psychiatry Now* . . . oh . . . and I've just finished *Gone with the Wind*.

POUND: *Gone with the Wind*?

WOMAN: By Margaret Mitchell.

POUND: Stepped in front of a bus, didn't she?

WOMAN: I think it was an automobile.

POUND: That's right. Hit and run. Some people have all the luck.

In a bizarre display of fatigue, POUND stretches out on the floor, placing his hands over his heart.

The WOMAN watches POUND, unsure how to respond. POUND twists and turns, trying to make himself as flat as possible.

WOMAN: Mr Pound. (PAUSE) Mr Pound?

He sits up.

POUND: There it is again!

WOMAN: What?

POUND: Did you hear that?

WOMAN: Hear what?

POUND: Someone laughing.

WOMAN: Where?

POUND: Sort of . . . (GESTURING) Sort of there!

The WOMAN listens.

WOMAN: I don't hear anything.

POUND: Shush!

WOMAN: It's probably one of the other patients . . .

POUND gets to his feet.

WOMAN: Or termites.

POUND: Nonsense! Termites don't laugh!

WOMAN: It's a very old building.

POUND: They laugh in old buildings?

WOMAN: Mr Pound . . .

POUND: I bet we'd be able to see them if I turned the lights out. Will I turn the lights out?

WOMAN: I'm sure that won't be necessary.

POUND: But you won't be able to see them with the lights on, not unless they light a match . . . and they're not allowed to smoke.

POUND moves toward the light switch.

WOMAN: (HUMORING HIM) No! Not in a theatre.

POUND: Now you're catching on!

POUND switches the lights off. DARKNESS.

WOMAN: Mr Pound! (PAUSE) Ouch!!

POUND: Sorry.

WOMAN: Mr Pound, where have you gone?

Chair noises, banging.

WOMAN: This is ridiculous.

POUND: Can you see them?

WOMAN: Who?

POUND: The people.

WOMAN: What people?

POUND: Give it a minute. Let the eyes adjust. Extraordinary what you can see once the eyes adjust.

WOMAN: I can't see a thing.

POUND: Patience, my dear . . .

WOMAN: Please turn on the lights, Mr Pound.

POUND: Oh yes, yes . . . I'm starting to see something now . . . over there . . . on the left.

WOMAN: I'm going to call the orderly, Mr Pound!

POUND: Wait!! Can't you see that?

WOMAN: Where?

POUND: You've got eyes don't you?

WOMAN: There's nothing to see.

The WOMAN switches on the lights. POUND is standing on top of his desk, hand over his eyes, staring out at the audience. He turns to the WOMAN.

POUND: What're you doing?

WOMAN: Would you mind coming down?

POUND: What for?

WOMAN: I want to talk to you.

POUND: Did you see them?

WOMAN: (ANGRILY) Would you *please* come down!

POUND: But there's a whole group of em.

WOMAN: I know.

POUND steps down onto a chair.

POUND: And they're watching us. *Both* of us.

WOMAN: Maybe if we mind our own business they'll go away.

POUND: No, I've tried that. It only encourages em.

POUND steps off the chair.

WOMAN: Well, why don't we encourage them a little more, then.

POUND: It's not like you think.

WOMAN: I'm sure.

POUND: (GLANCING TOWARD THE AUDIENCE) Maggots!

WOMAN: Sit down, Mr Pound.

POUND sits.

WOMAN: Thank you. (SHE SITS) The Justice Department is reviewing your case for the purpose of ascertaining your mental competency. They've authorised me to make an assessment. Based on my findings and the doctors' reports, a recommendation will be made about your fitness to answer the charges against you.

POUND: Usual bureaucratic balls-up, eh?

WOMAN: Routine procedure.

POUND: Probably would've been easier if I'd hung myself!

WOMAN: The government wants your case settled one way or the other. That's why I'm here.

POUND: Well, what's it been now? Eleven, twelve years? And still no trial. I'd say you haven't come a moment too soon.

WOMAN: You were the one who pleaded insanity.

POUND: Bad legal advice. (BEAT) Do I look like I have a screw loose?

POUND smiles. The WOMAN blinks back in silence.

WOMAN: Treason is punishable by death, Mr Pound.

POUND: So is life, my dear.

WOMAN: They can still send you to the electric chair, you know.

POUND: I ain't skeerd.

WOMAN: You understand what I'm saying.

POUND: Oh yes, I understand plenty. It's all that other crap the law doesn't cover that confuses me.

WOMAN: Such as?

POUND: The sanctified stupidities! The whole structure of what we so glibly refer to as civilisation. What about all that?

WOMAN: What about it?

POUND: You tell me.

WOMAN: What do you want me to say?

POUND: Just tell the truth.

WOMAN: The Committee's judging you, Mr Pound. Society isn't part of the brief.

POUND: Oh I see. Yes! That explains everything. Of course. The memo mentality. Cogs in the wheel. Right. I almost forgot. "Whom God would destroy, he first puts into the hands of the public service!" Silly me. Silly old fart. I actually thought poetry could make a difference in the world. My mistake. Obviously it is the brief writers who have the power in this country. I was merely succinct.

WOMAN: This hasn't anything to do with poetry, Mr Pound.

POUND: No, goddammit, it's about usury and decay.

The destruction of everything Adams and Jefferson stood for. The nation's wealth reduced to interest payments, and managed by a few individuals for private profit without any kind of production whatsoever. Greed before bread. Mediocrity cloaked in graft.

WOMAN: The question is whether or not you are capable of defending yourself.

POUND: You mean am I crazy.

WOMAN: If it's decided that your mental faculties are such that you can mount a reasonable defense, then you'll have your day in court.

POUND: And if I'm nuts?

WOMAN: Then you will have to remain here.

POUND: Well I ain't guilty and the bastards know it! The only reason they keep me cooped up is so I can't tell the truth about em.

WOMAN: Some of your descriptions of President Roosevelt were pretty extreme. People aren't likely to forget that sort of thing.

POUND: I only said what was true.

WOMAN: Over the radio.

POUND: And what about freedom of speech? Or don't that apply to poets no more?

WOMAN: The Constitution applies to everyone, Mr Pound.

POUND: Well, freedom of speech is a mockery if it don't include free speech over the radio.

WOMAN: Freedom of speech doesn't mean you can say anything you like.

POUND: The theatre was on fire, my dear!

WOMAN: You said the country was run by pigs.

POUND: I only gave em the facts.

WOMAN: As you saw them.

POUND: As an American citizen!

WOMAN: You defended Fascism.

POUND: My talks gave pain to the enemy . . . the *real* enemy.

WOMAN: I've read the transcripts, Mr Pound.

POUND: Then you had better read them again.

WOMAN: You said what you said during wartime.

POUND: To save the Constitution.

WOMAN: By undermining the government?

POUND: By trying to bust a racket! You think we elect the people who run this country? Political bugwash. It's private interest that runs this country. I tell you, there's a conspiracy against decency and justice going on out there, and it's going on right now!

WOMAN: Hitler and Mussolini were the conspirators.

POUND: Bilge!

WOMAN: You think they cared about decency and justice? The history of America was made by men who gave their lives to fight that kind of hatred and intolerance.

POUND: The history of this country was made by men who kept their names out of it so's they wouldn't be caught.

WOMAN: I don't believe that.

POUND: Believe what you like. A man still has the right to defend himself, to have his ideas examined one at a time.

The WOMAN stares back at him, then looks

down and consults her notepad.

WOMAN: I understand you're a close friend of the novelist . . . James Joyce.

POUND: Ah yes. Joyce and I speak regularly.

WOMAN: He lives in Washington?

POUND: No. No. As a matter of fact, he's dead.

WOMAN: I'm sorry.

POUND: These things happen.

WOMAN: Nevertheless, there seem to be a number of living writers who see you as the most important literary figure of the twentieth century.

POUND: And no one believes em!

WOMAN: Ernest Hemingway says you taught him everything he knows about writing. T.S. Eliot refers to you as a genius.

POUND: Where's it say that?

WOMAN: They've signed a petition. The one Robert Frost was sending round. They're calling you the father of modern poetry.

POUND: It does have a ring about it, doesn't it?

WOMAN: Yes.

POUND: And what damn good has it done?

WOMAN: You're almost a household name.

POUND: That's what my wife says.

WOMAN: You're famous.

POUND: A smidgen of a reputation, my dear; nothing to get excited about. Nothing approaching that of Mr Eisenhower's in any case.

WOMAN: President Eisenhower isn't a writer.

POUND: No, not yet, but I'm sure he's working on it.

At least he can get to a good library when he needs one. By the way, how's the golf game?

WOMAN: Still shooting in the low 90s, I believe.

POUND: Good! Great game, golf. Impossible, though, in a room this size.

The WOMAN scribbles a note in her pad. POUND cranes his neck to watch.

POUND: (REMINDING HER) "... room this size."

WOMAN: Thank you.

POUND: Don't mention it.

The WOMAN watches as POUND moves slowly to his bed. He lies down.

WOMAN: Doctor Barnes has been a little disturbed.

POUND: You've noticed?

WOMAN: He thinks you talk in circles.

POUND: Graphic imagination, that boy.

WOMAN: He believes you are suffering from some kind of severe self-deception.

POUND: Cat-piss!

WOMAN: You don't like Doctor Barnes, do you?

POUND: (WITH ACCENT) Waal ... let's just say he ain't as entertainin' as Elvis Presley.

WOMAN: He's assembled quite an impressive amount of data concerning your case.

POUND: Barnes is a scientist. He believes everything can be reduced to numbers.

WOMAN: Doctor Barnes is also a highly qualified doctor.

POUND: He equates health with servility.

WOMAN: He was saying that you talk in your sleep.

He said you do it almost every night.

POUND: Last bastion of free speech in this country, my dear.

WOMAN: At first, he thought it was only gibberish. But now he has the impression you were mumbling names.

POUND sits up.

POUND: Names? What sort of names?

WOMAN: He thought they sounded foreign. You speak several languages, don't you?

POUND: I can ask for the bathroom in Latin if that's what you mean.

POUND pulls an apple from the bedclothes. He begins polishing it on his sleeve as the WOMAN consults her notepad, flicking through the pages until she's found what she's looking for.

WOMAN: What does Wool-long-gong* mean to you?

POUND: Come again.

WOMAN: (READING) Wool-long-gong.

POUND: Is it supposed to mean something?

WOMAN: You tell me.

POUND: (THINKING) Woollen gong . . . Woollen gong. What a strange concept.

WOMAN: Why is that?

POUND: A woollen gong! You wouldn't be able to hear it.

The WOMAN stares back, then consults her pad again.

WOMAN: What about . . . (READS) Warr-nam-bool?

---

* phonetically denotes Wollongong — a town in NSW

POUND: Warr-nam-bool . . . Warrnambool. No, I don't think I know this language.

WOMAN: (READS) Wand-jina.

POUND: Wand-jina?

WOMAN: That's what it says . . . (SPELLING IT) W-A-N-D- . . .

POUND: What is this? Verbal ink blots?

WOMAN: They're some of the words you've been mumbling in your sleep. The orderly, Mr Brierson, wrote them down.

POUND: Brierson!

WOMAN: He thought they might be part of a code.

POUND: God! I wish he'd find a hobby.

WOMAN: They're not code words?

POUND: My dear woman, our greatest problem is that almost everything is a goddamned code. We do not know what is real any more. Every gesture is symbolic. A man cannot shit short of some pundit discovering hidden meaning in it. Even having children is a metaphor. Hence, we cannot trust ourselves; and therefore, we do not trust anyone. No, my dear, I do not believe in codes and even if I did I certainly would not use one in my sleep!

POUND takes a bite from his apple.

WOMAN: Doctor Barnes thinks they may be the names of places in Australia.

POUND: Auss'ralia?

WOMAN: That's what he said. You made several references to Australia in the radio broadcasts. You suggested selling it to the Jews, I believe.

POUND: Barnes has been to Auss'ralia, has he?

WOMAN: Not that I know of.

POUND: How the hell would he know then?

WOMAN: I believe he found them in his crossword puzzle dictionary.

POUND: That'd be right. Mind like a steel trap.

WOMAN: Do you do crosswords?

POUND: Not if I can help it. Now that you mention it, though, I do remember Barnes asking me for a seven-letter word starting with 'B' . . . the name for an Auss'ralian wild horse.

WOMAN: And . . .?

POUND: I called him a bastard . . . and he wrote that down!

WOMAN: You've never been to Australia?

POUND: Not as I can recall. (BEAT) I read *The Edge*.

WOMAN: The edge?

POUND: It's an Auss'ralian literary journal.

WOMAN: Really?

POUND: They *can* read, y'know.

WOMAN: Of course. It's just that . . . well . . . whenever I think about Australia, well . . . I think of kangaroos and deserts . . . and . . . and sheep. It's always seemed so large and empty and faraway.

POUND: Idaho is worse.

WOMAN: But Idaho is connected to something bigger.

POUND: So is Auss'ralia . . . under the ocean.

The WOMAN makes more notes in her pad.

POUND goes to his desk and picks up a pair of binoculars. He examines them, then holds them up to his eyes, adjusting the focus. He gazes toward the audience, then takes them away from his eyes. He shakes them and looks again.

POUND: Damned things are permanently out of focus! (EXAMINING THEM) Government issue.

The WOMAN observes POUND for a moment. He has another look, then lowers the binoculars and turns to her.

POUND: The illusion of vistas, my dear. Have a look.

He offers them to her, but she doesn't respond.

POUND: Maybe it was something I ate . . .

WOMAN: Something you ate?

POUND: This talking in my sleep . . . maybe it's the food.

WOMAN: Or something from your past.

POUND: Hmmm . . .

WOMAN: Tell me about Australia. What do you know about it?

POUND: Not much.

WOMAN: What've you heard, then; what have you read?

POUND: I can't see what this has to do with my mental competency.

WOMAN: It is interesting, though, don't you think? The names you've been saying.

POUND: What comes out of the mouth doesn't necessarily explain anything . . . although . . . (A PRIVATE REALISATION) Ahhh!

A PAUSE.

WOMAN: What?

POUND: Never mind. It's not important.

WOMAN: Tell me.

POUND: No, I've talked too much.

WOMAN: But we haven't even started.

POUND: We haven't?

WOMAN: Tell me what you were going to say.

POUND sits down next to the WOMAN.

POUND: Ever walked naked in a desert?

WOMAN: Pardon me?

POUND: You know . . . taken off your clothes and walked naked . . . in a desert.

WOMAN: Are you serious?

POUND: I knew you wouldn't understand.

WOMAN: You're not making yourself very clear.

POUND: That's the problem. Words cannot do everything. You'd have to have been there.

WOMAN: Where?

POUND: (SIGHS) Find a desert, take off your clothes and walk! The sense of vulnerability is exhilarating. To feel the wind on your skin; the hot sand on the soles of your feet. To be part of the Earth.

WOMAN: I'm a Methodist.

POUND: Methodists, Jews, Taoists . . . it hardly matters, my dear.

WOMAN: I had a grandmother who was a nudist.

POUND: Good gawd!

WOMAN: Oh, I shouldn't have said that. We promised we'd never tell anyone outside the family. I mean

... well ... we all thought of her as the black sheep, but ...

POUND: Don't apologise.

WOMAN: I wasn't apologising!

POUND: Sounded like it.

WOMAN: Well I wasn't.

POUND: Good. (BEAT) You wouldn't happen to be against the death penalty by any chance, would you?

WOMAN: We're not here to talk about me, Mr Pound.

POUND: No. No, of course not. How rude of me. It's just that when you mentioned your grandmother ...

WOMAN: We were talking about Australia.

POUND: Yes, Auss'ralia. (BEAT) Auss'ralia?

WOMAN: Tell me about it.

POUND: Whaddaya wanna hear?

WOMAN: Whatever you like.

POUND: Auss'ralia, eh? (THINKS) Waal ... it's, uh, it's the oldest piece of dry land on earth.

WOMAN: Yes.

POUND: And, uh ... it has a parliamentary democracy.

WOMAN: Uh-huh.

POUND: It gave women the vote years before the Americans even thought of it ... and ...

WOMAN: Go on.

POUND: And, uh ... it's the home of the Pintupi.

WOMAN: The what?

POUND: Did I say that?

WOMAN: You said home of the . . . something.

POUND: Home of the Pintupi. An obscure Aboriginal tribe.

WOMAN: You know about the Aborigines.

POUND: There is a reference or two in *The Pisan Cantos*.

WOMAN: You've written about them.

POUND: Oh yes.

WOMAN: That's strange. There's no mention of that in your file.

POUND: There is now.

WOMAN: (BEAT) Tell me more.

POUND: It's not all in books, my dear.

WOMAN: So . . .

POUND: So imagine: no books, no libraries, no bank accounts, no clothes! You wanna know where civilisation screws up? It wears clothes when it should be naked and is naked when it should be wearing clothes. Europe, for example.

WOMAN: Europe?

POUND: Ah yes, Yoo-rup! How wonderfully plump!
Gluttonous to the core!
Force-fed and filled-up from early infantry
to *Murder in the Cathedral*.
Conceived out of cave men and cave women!
Terrorised by sabre tooth and frost;
devoid of pulchritude.
Familiar and strange as the parts
of one's body one never sees.
Or the eyes of eagles lost
in machines evolved from earth
and trees in the heartland
of indolent factories . . .

WOMAN: Mr Pound . . .

POUND stands.

POUND: Battalions of concerti;
brigades of ballerinas;
vast armies of sculptures,
bastion-like with retinues of scribes
and chanting. Crowded in,
backs against the weather.
Crowding — a goad for competition.
Fighting makes the blood hot, you know.
And makes the bankers even richer.
Two thousand years of kulchur
to make a habit of Art!

The WOMAN makes a note in her pad.

POUND: And what have we actually produced? Corruption. Bankruptcy. Wars. The higher maggotry! Not like the Aborigines!

POUND picks up the apple. He snaps off another chunk and tosses the core over his shoulder.

WOMAN: Was that one of your own compositions?

POUND: You liked it?

WOMAN: Not particularly. Was it a poem?

POUND: No.

WOMAN: It sounded like a poem.

POUND: I make it a point never to write poems while I'm being interviewed.

WOMAN: It was very passionate.

POUND: Thank you.

WOMAN: And a little frightening.

POUND: You're fishing.

WOMAN: You know, I think Australia might be a very important key to unlocking what's inside of you.

POUND: What about what's outside of me?

WOMAN: Australia was a prison colony, wasn't it?

POUND: The English sent their children there for stealing loaves of bread.

WOMAN: It must have been horrible.

POUND: The British have always had an interest in prisons. Building them, I mean. Industrious little buggers with an obsession for security.

WOMAN: Maybe that's the connection.

POUND: What?

WOMAN: Maybe you see some parallel between Australia and your time here.

POUND: No. Too obvious.

WOMAN: But it's not impossible.

POUND: Nothing's impossible, my dear.

A PAUSE.

WOMAN: Do you ever dream?

POUND: (WITH SUSPICION) Why?

WOMAN: You were having a dream when I came in, weren't you?

POUND: *After* you came in.

WOMAN: Can you remember it?

POUND: This part of the investigation?

WOMAN: Does it make you nervous?

POUND: Should it?

WOMAN: You tell me.

POUND: Reckon I might let something slip, eh?

WOMAN: I shouldn't think so.

POUND: You following all this?

WOMAN: So far.

POUND: Good.

WOMAN: Can you remember any of your dreams?

POUND: How do you know I won't just make something up?

WOMAN: I don't.

POUND: Waal . . . there is one, one that recurs. Quite odd, really.

WOMAN: Is it always the same?

POUND: Always the same . . . more or less.

WOMAN: Tell me about it.

POUND: Well, uh . . . let me see . . . there's, uh, red earth . . . and, uh, stone implements. Axeheads, that sort of thing . . . on the ground. And, uh, a mountainous horizon . . . strange-looking trees . . . silence. (BEAT) Oh yeah . . . and rabbit shit.

WOMAN: Pardon me?

POUND: Well I'm no expert, but it's about the right size.

WOMAN: Is it vivid?

POUND: The rabbit shit?

WOMAN: The dream.

POUND: No, not vivid, no . . . more like seeing everything through a smoke haze. Where do you suppose they come from?

WOMAN: Dreams?

POUND: Refresh my memory . . . that is what we're talking about, isn't it?

WOMAN: It's a difficult question.

POUND: I'm not going anywhere.

WOMAN: Oh, I thought you said you were busy.

POUND: You've changed my mind.

WOMAN: I see. Well . . . I've always thought of dreams as an expression of an individual's unacted desires and urges. Repressed emotions and drives are symbolically lived out in dream states . . . The entire history of the human race, theoretically, can be understood in terms of repression. The conscious mind is only a very small part of the total picture. In civilised societies, we find these repressed urges bubbling up in dreams. They may not be . . . (PAUSE) Are you listening, Mr Pound?

POUND: The Freudian angle, eh?

WOMAN: You don't agree with Freud?

POUND: We spend twelve hundred generations developing so-called civilisation to the point where it produces an expert who can offer us salvation from our superstitions and all we end up with is another superstition. If it takes someone like Freud to save us from our neuroses, what's it going to take to save us from Freud?

WOMAN: Oh, I get it. Freud. Of course. He's Jewish. Freud's Jewish and you think the Jews . . .

POUND: I thought we were talking dreams.

WOMAN: We are.

POUND: "Viennese sewage! America's been up Freud's asshole for twenty years."

WOMAN: But the fact that he's Jewish . . .

POUND: "PussyKIKEeatrists! The conspiracy of Jews is responsible for everything wrong with the world, including the publishing business! Read *The*

28

Protocols. The Ten Commandments is 'Chewlaw'. A lot of regulations not based on any ethic whatsodam but merely aimed at imposing fines fer the benefit of priests and levys. The jew book has been filling bughouses with nuts ever since they set up such institutions."

WOMAN: That's a very harsh assessment.

POUND: What they've done to mankind is worse.

WOMAN: You had a lot to say about them in the radio broadcasts.

POUND: I wouldn't hurt a fly.

The WOMAN consults her notepad.

WOMAN: On the ninth of April, 1942, you said that ". . . the United States has been invaded by vermin, meaning the Jews, and that Roosevelt belonged in an insane asylum . . ."

POUND: Too good for him.

WOMAN: On the twenty-third of April, you told your audience that "If the American public had had the sense to eliminate Roosevelt and his Jews or the Jews and their Roosevelt at the last election, America would've never gone to war."

POUND: They've known for years what I think about em.

WOMAN: You have signed letters with "Heil Hitler" and swastikas. You've even described Hitler as a saint and a martyr. (BEAT) Do you hate the Jews that much?

POUND: As a whole, no. No, on the whole I have a bigger quarrel with the Irish. But I can't see what any of this has to do with the indictment. I wasn't indicted for anti-semitism, was I?

WOMAN: No.

POUND: Well, I'm glad we agree on that.

WOMAN: You knew what you were saying, though, didn't you?

POUND: No one understood a damn thing.

WOMAN: But you knew what you were saying.

A PAUSE.

POUND: Yes.

WOMAN: Do you really hate them that much?

POUND: One must take them individually, my dear.

WOMAN: Not like they were taken at Auschwitz, you mean.

A PAUSE.

POUND: There weren't any gas ovens in Italy.

WOMAN: And not very much justice, either.

POUND: Ask the Rothschilds about justice.

WOMAN: And what about the Cohens . . . and the Blums . . . and the Goldsteins?

POUND: Friends of yours, are they?

WOMAN: You seem to have a preoccupation with tribal people.

POUND: My mind wanders. Nomad. (MORE EMPHATIC) Nomad!

WOMAN: You think life would've been more bearable if the brown shirts had taken over.

POUND: That's got nothing to do with it. And stop telling me what I think!

WOMAN: I'm trying to understand you, Mr Pound.

POUND: Well, you'll not understand a damn thing until you understand the money system. How many times do I have to say it?

WOMAN: Getting angry isn't going to help.

POUND: "FIVE million young people without jobs.
One hundred thousand violent crimes.
FOUR million adult illiterates.
THIRD term of FDR
CASE for the prosecution."

WOMAN: You could say that about a lot of countries.

POUND: But not the richest country in the world.

WOMAN: It's not as simple as that.

POUND: The truth is always simple. It's only the Lie that is complicated.

WOMAN: And you have the answers?

POUND: No country can suppress truth and live well.

WOMAN: And what about patriotism? What about loyalty? Don't they count for anything?

POUND: Oh, I'm all for national pride, my dear. You know me. But you're a fool if you think you can have loyalty to something you don't understand. The horror is: those in power know even less about what's going on than I do! Or you do! So long as the papers arrive every morning and the toast doesn't burn, we are quite content to believe it all has meaning. Life in the monkeyhouse.

WOMAN: You're very lucky, you know, being an American citizen. In another country, they would've thrown away the key.

POUND: Yes, in a free country they keep dangling it in front of your face, just out of reach.

WOMAN: At least we have equality and freedom of choice.

POUND: Oh yes! Too many choices, too many pies, too many digits, tho' a finite number of thumbs and fingers; ergo: apple, peach and punkin — even the thought of em — don't seem to satisfy. (BEAT) America should have lost the war. Look how the Japs prosper!

WOMAN: You are unhappy about the result of the war?

POUND: "The trouble with modern warfare is that it never gives you a chance to kill the right people." And yes, I am unhappy. (PAUSE) Do you fancy a cup of tea?

WOMAN: No thank you.

POUND: Good. Nothing so undramatic as a cup of tea. (BEAT) What about a bagel, then?

WOMAN: Nothing.

POUND: Provolone?

WOMAN: I'm not hungry.

POUND: For anything?

WOMAN: I've eaten.

POUND: Maybe there's nothing to do but give up speaking altogether. I should have taken my day in court when I had the chance.

The WOMAN makes a note in her pad. POUND cranes his neck to see what she is writing.

POUND: Your pen's leaking.

The WOMAN looks up. A PAUSE.

WOMAN: Are you satisfied with the treatment you've been receiving here?

POUND: What treatment?

WOMAN: The counselling, the care . . .

POUND: The bastards haven't even arrived at a diagnosis!

WOMAN: You have feelings of melancholia?

POUND: Unmitigated.

WOMAN: Fits of depression?

POUND: In abundance!

WOMAN: A sense of isolation?

POUND: It's not exactly the YMCA, is it?

WOMAN: You don't feel at home in America?

POUND: I live in an insane asylum. Of course I feel at home.

WOMAN: That's not what I meant.

POUND: Well, you can spend a lifetime getting clear about what you mean.

WOMAN: What do you want, Mr Pound?

POUND: A new civilisation.

A PROFOUND SILENCE.

WOMAN: If you were acquitted, would you stay in the United States?

POUND: And go to football games . . . and the World Series?

WOMAN: Yes.

POUND: (GETTING INTO IT) And sing the Star-Spangled Banner . . . and eat turkey and cranberry sauce at Thanksgiving . . . and television . . .?

WOMAN: I suppose.

POUND: "Oh! (RISING) Oh, the thought of what America / the thought of what America / the thought of what America would be like if the Classics had a wide circulation troubles my sleep!"

The WOMAN, somewhat taken aback, gazes at him.

WOMAN: I take it that means no.

POUND: I don't see that it's anyone's damn business what I do when I get out.

WOMAN: There's some concern that your criticisms of the United States might be exploited by a foreign power.

POUND: Which goes to show how little they know about history. I certainly don't feel like going anywhere. Not until I get my say.

WOMAN: You can say whatever you like.

POUND: In court!

WOMAN: You had the chance. You pleaded insanity.

POUND: I hadn't realised before what a compliment it was to be hanged.

WOMAN: The psychiatrists' reports from the detention centre in Pisa said you were sane.

POUND: And no one listened to em.

POUND rests his wrists on the clothesline 'filing system' in a posture resembling Christ on the cross.

WOMAN: You're very clever, aren't you? You say you want to go to court, and yet . . . you have everything you want right here. Wine, chess, caviar, tennis, a constant stream of visitors . . .

POUND: Yes. Everything except freedom.

WOMAN: Doctor Barnes says you're writing more than ever. It's not really so very different from being on a literary fellowship, is it?

POUND moves away from the clothesline.

POUND: I've always said America owed its ten best poets a living, but this wasn't exactly what I had in mind. (PAUSE) You'd like to see me get the chair, wouldn't you?

WOMAN: No.

POUND: Of course you would!

WOMAN: That's not so.

POUND: Think I've got it coming, eh?

WOMAN: It's not up to me.

POUND: (FRAMING THE WORDS WITH HIS HANDS) She always gets her man.

WOMAN: Look, I don't agree with what you've done, and a lot of what you say I find completely despicable, but I don't believe in capital punishment, either. That's what makes this so difficult.

POUND: Yes. A bitch of a situation.

WOMAN: We're talking about your life, Mr Pound.

POUND: We're talking about the rights of the individual.

WOMAN: The individual doesn't always come first.

POUND: What'd they have to do to buy you off?

WOMAN: No one's bought me.

POUND: Then why're you going against what you believe?

WOMAN: Sometimes the national interest is more important.

POUND: And whose interest is that . . . specifically?

WOMAN: Anyone who loves his country.

POUND: A human being has a duty to avoid servility.

WOMAN: Sometimes people abuse freedom.

POUND: Only when they ain't free.

A BEAT.

WOMAN: You're not a political prisoner, Mr Pound.

POUND: No, I'm here for committing accuracy.

WOMAN: You threatened the United States.

POUND: Just the cranks who were running it.

A PAUSE.

WOMAN: I think you like it here. The noble victim, the abused visionary, the genius in the madhouse. That offers you a lot more scope than the role of the elderly, almost-forgotten poet in exile, doesn't it?

POUND: It's heartening to see you're not letting objectivity obscure the issues.

WOMAN: You're the centre of attention here. Living proof of the injustice of the system. You don't really want to be released, do you? You've been using us all along.

POUND: I certainly have not dropped an atom bomb on anyone.

WOMAN: The bomb was used to *stop* the war.

POUND: The bomb was used so's they'd have somethin to show for the two million bucks they spent.

WOMAN: If you hadn't been a poet — if you'd been a doctor or a lawyer or even a factory worker — no voice would've been raised in your defense. But if the court finds you guilty, you're guilty twice — for treason as a citizen and for the poet's betrayal of everything that is decent in human civilisation.

POUND: Go on, say it! Old Ez is as nutty as a fruitcake. That's what you think.

WOMAN: (CALMLY) No I don't.

POUND: Yes you do.

WOMAN: (EVENLY) I do not.

POUND: That's what America thinks . . . *if* it thinks.

WOMAN: You're acting like a child.

POUND: Maybe we can organise a guillotine instead of a hanging.

SILENCE. The WOMAN considers POUND with new eyes.

WOMAN: You don't want this to go to court, do you?

POUND: The question is: am I right?

WOMAN: The question is: are you sane? I don't think you're as crazy as everyone thinks.

POUND: Oh, they're going to love hearing that down at the Justice Department. Locking up a sane man in an asylum for nearly thirteen years; yes, that sounds like the American Way.

WOMAN: I'm not a fool, Mr Pound.

POUND: Then stop acting like one.

WOMAN: I beg your pardon.

POUND: You heard me.

WOMAN: Stop it!

POUND: What're you afraid of?

WOMAN: Not you.

POUND: What then?

WOMAN: Nothing.

POUND: I don't believe you.

WOMAN: I don't care.

POUND: Of course you do.

WOMAN: Why should I?

POUND: Even the language fights against me!

WOMAN: What do you want me to say?

POUND: It does seem a bit curious don't you think? You, coming down here, asking me all these questions?

WOMAN: I don't know what you're talking about.

POUND: Maybe there's something going on behind your back. Ever thought of that?

WOMAN: I don't think so.

POUND: Maybe it's a set-up.

WOMAN: A set-up?

POUND: Maybe they're using you for something. (BEAT) Yes! That's it! That's exactly what it is!

WOMAN: Mr Pound . . .

POUND: Can't you see it? They're not interested in how I am . . . who I am . . . or even what I am. All they're concerned about is getting themselves off the hook with a minimum of fuss. (BEAT) They've got us both exactly where they want us!

WOMAN: What!?

POUND: Sending you down here to this dreary rat-trap, making you listen to a crazy old fool. I'll bet they're not even paying you what you're worth.

WOMAN: Money has nothing to do with it.

POUND: Don't believe it.

WOMAN: Not for me.

POUND: No?

WOMAN: Not at all.

POUND: You sure?

WOMAN: Yes.

POUND: Positive?

WOMAN: Yes!

A PAUSE.

POUND: All right then, sling us fifty bucks.

POUND smiles.

WOMAN: I'm glad you find me so amusing.

POUND: Bottom of the totem pole, eh? New kid on the block.

WOMAN: You don't know what you're talking about.

POUND: Course I don't. I'm paranoid and depressed and untrustworthy! But think about it: you're the sucker making the recommendations . . .

WOMAN: The Department isn't out to get you, Mr Pound.

POUND: No, it's *you* they're after!

A PAUSE.

WOMAN: That's ridiculous.

POUND: Say I'm mad and they'll have to leave me here. America's skeleton in the closet, the national treasure it deserves. But if you say I'm sane you'll have to give me the forum of a courtroom, you'll have to let me speak . . . and maybe, even, the firing squad. You wouldn't like that, would you? No, my dear, we're both on trial here.

WOMAN: I don't believe that for a minute.

POUND: And that's exactly what will allow them to get away with it!

WOMAN: Get away with what?

POUND: The lies! The treachery! The hypocrisy!

WOMAN: Your mental condition is what we're interested in.

POUND: Like shit it is! This is about justice and injustice. The right to confide or not to confide. To decide what we give away, and what we keep.

WOMAN: Why are you talking like this?

POUND: Because I want to know what is mine! (BEAT) How far do you people go?

WOMAN: I'm only doing my job.

POUND: Oh yes . . . a real team player.

WOMAN: A loyal citizen.

POUND: Loyal to fragments.

WOMAN: Loyal to my government . . . to democracy . . . to the values that America stands for!

POUND: Baloney! We're talking about the powers of light and darkness, here. To have allegiance to what is scattered is usury. By god, how they tempt us! (BEAT) You should never have taken this on, y'know. You should've stayed right out of it.

WOMAN: I think I'm capable of looking after myself.

POUND: I'll bet nobody else wanted it.

WOMAN: Nobody else was asked.

POUND: That's right! Because this situation . . . this forgotten piece of the war . . . this demented old porcupine is a bitch of an embarrassment to them, and it has nothing to do with my mental health. This is about the abuse of language; it's an exercise in face-saving and scapegoating . . . and you're it!

A PAUSE.

WOMAN: Maybe you're right, maybe we are both on trial. So what do I do? Tell them you're sane and give you the opportunity to speak, knowing they won't listen, and knowing that they'll probably execute you; or lie about your mental condition and leave you here?

POUND: Would you lie about something like that?

WOMAN: I have never lied in my life.

POUND: Yes . . . a Methodist.

The WOMAN opens her briefcase, puts her pad and pencil inside, and snaps it shut.

POUND: Where are you going?

WOMAN: Home.

POUND: Home!? But what about *my* questions?

WOMAN: What questions are those?

POUND: Well, it's been a bit one-sided, don't you think? A bit of a one-way street.

WOMAN: Maybe next time.

POUND: There might not be a next time. I may never see you again. There are things you can tell me.

WOMAN: I doubt it.

She turns to leave.

POUND: You call this justice? (BEAT) Wait!

She stops.

POUND: All right. All right, I know I've been difficult but . . .

WOMAN: You've been abysmal! (PAUSE) You have no idea what it's like . . . always having to prove I can do the job, that I'm as good as any man. They expect me to fail, you know, but I'm not going to! I'm as good as any of them, and better than most.

POUND: You take them too seriously.

WOMAN: What did you do?

A MOMENT.

POUND: I am sure we will remember the fifties with a great deal more fondness than we felt while living through them.

WOMAN: They said you'd be difficult. But I came along today with an open mind. (BEAT) You may despise what I represent, and I guess you're entitled to despise it given the fact you've been locked away here all these years. But that doesn't give you the right to insult me! You think you're the only person who's ever been persecuted? Do you really believe that the poetry legitimises what you've done and said? Well, it doesn't. And it never will. I may not be an artist or a poet, like you, but I have feelings too, and they can be hurt.

POUND: I'd wager the Department doesn't know what it's got, having you on the payroll.

WOMAN: On the contrary, that's why I got your case!

POUND: I'm honoured.

The WOMAN stiffens, trying to control her anger. She explodes.

WOMAN: You smug, self-congratulating old fascist! You think you're so smart, don't you? Even after twelve years in this hole, you still think you know more than everyone else. The poor, misunderstood genius. The helpless victim who believes he has all the answers if only the world would listen to him. But a coward's still a coward no matter what he hides behind, and poetry won't change that. You're wrong and you know you're wrong. Mussolini was a tyrant. Hitler was a butcher! And there are probably just as many poor Jews out there who have been done in by the banks as anyone else. But in your world you only use the ingredients that suit you. Well . . . as far as this public servant is concerned, you can go straight to hell!

She turns away from him, overcome by emotion. POUND *sits on the edge of his bed.*

SILENCE.

She turns back.

WOMAN: Mr Pound.

SILENCE.

WOMAN: Mr Pound?

SILENCE.

WOMAN: Mr Pound?

SILENCE.

WOMAN: Mr Pound.

SILENCE.

WOMAN: This won't help you, you know. Sooner or later you'll have to speak.

SILENCE.

WOMAN: Mr Pound?

No reply.

WOMAN: Mr Pound . . . ?

SILENCE. *She sits down beside him on the bed.*

WOMAN: (GENTLY SHAKING HIM) Mr Pound . . . where are you?

He slowly turns to her.

POUND: "Why . . . in hell, my dear. In hell!"

They regard each other for a moment.

WOMAN: I guess there's nothing more to say.

POUND: Everyone is alone. That is what our culture has produced — a pain deeper than politics.

WOMAN: So what am I supposed to do?

POUND: That's the wrong question.

WOMAN: What're we supposed to do?

POUND: Let's not turn this into a farce.

WOMAN: I agree.

POUND: We're not ignorant people. We're not dumb animals.

WOMAN: You're a very difficult man, Mr Pound.

POUND: Yes, my dear, I know. A real challenge.

POUND moves closer to the WOMAN.

POUND: So . . . tell me about *Gone with the Wind*.

STAGE LIGHTS OUT.

END ACT ONE

ACT TWO

POUND'S room. If anything, it is messier than before.

POUND hums tunelessly to himself as he sorts through the chaos of books, manuscripts and assorted scraps of junk that clutter his living quarters. He retrieves what he wants and variously disposes of those items that hold no interest. His movements suggest some kind of inner logic. Is he getting ready for trial or preparing himself for the death house? Is this a prelude to freedom or the gallows? A beginning or an end?

He extracts a few articles of clothing from a dresser drawer: a sweater, a shirt, a bathrobe. He folds these haphazardly and places them on a chair near the foot of his bed. Several books are caught up in the bedclothes. He picks these up, weighs them in both hands, then selects two volumes which he places on his desk. The others are stacked on the floor.

He moves around his desk, stopping to peer at the sheet of paper in his typewriter. He reads what is written there, pauses a moment, then types a line. He reads it silently to himself. Satisfied, he turns, surveying the room — what next?

He unpegs several sheets of manuscript from his clothesline. Some of these he places on a small table; others go into the rubbish bin. [NOTE: This is happening as the audience returns from intermission.]

HOUSE LIGHTS DOWN.

POUND continues working, putting his house in order, discarding some items, retaining others. He returns to his typewriter and types another line, then he sorts through another stack of books. He places a few more volumes on his desk, and types another line. He pulls the sheet of paper from the typewriter, examining the results of his latest re-write.

POUND: (READING)
    Sic semper tyrannis,
    a brackish tribulation.
    The knowledge of plants and birds
    serves better than a stipend.
    A direct feeling . . .
    (WEIGHING THE WORDS)
    A direct feeling . . .

POUND becomes aware of a presence in his room. He squints, shading his eyes with his hand.

What?! Oh. You again! Can't get enough, eh?
Enjoying the nuthouse, are we?
(WADDING UP THE PAPER)
Government by the peep-hole, of the peep-hole,
for the peep-hole.
(TOSSING THE PAPER OVER HIS SHOULDER)
"A cage": the metaphor too obvious, too
    alliterative,
didactic, humourless;
tho' useful on occasion.
Leaden diadem of the banking mentality:
Paying one's debt to society.
Life in the monkeyhouse.
Not such a good place for poetry, but . . .
"no man has perennial fortune,
slow foot, or swift foot, death delays
but for a season."

POUND follows the flight of a fly through the air. He reaches for a manuscript and holds it at the ready. The fly lights on his typewriter. He observes it for a moment before slamming the manuscript down. He examines the flattened insect, then flicks it.

Better to say: 'Montana is in the air.'
'Big sky ceiling.'
A walk through deserted streets
of one's childhood home.
The joke is on me.

He moves slowly DOWNSTAGE. His manner is conversational at first, as if addressing someone in the audience, and becomes more dramatic as he warms up.

How long have you been in?
(BEAT) I see. You're not in.
That's what they all say.
You're not . . . going anywhere though, are you?
Yes, I understand.
Capisce!
Never the proposals that get in the way;
only the stupid questions,
and inattention to answers;
the blind assent to speed;
the headlong rush into untried truth
because he said this
and she said that,
so long as everything is quick;
so long as everything is sweet.
As if Life could be conceived
and born in a night's sleep;
toddling by breakfast;
high school on the way to work;
college and a perfect marriage by noon;
old age for lunch; and a palsied decline
in time for tea . . .
setting for an early hour

the alarm clock by Death;
and Heaven: another sleep.
So how is it that Men and Women
make it through another day
with such velocity,
with so little deliberation?
(PAUSE)
Freedom is a wishbone
caught up in the hand of a child who
believes in magic and cannot speak,
for speaking does not make wishes happen.
What is closest to us must always remain a secret,
and there is tragedy in this.
Syntax cannot change this room.
Something more is required . . .
or something less.
Courage: the rudimentary ingredient.
Better to reflect the world without a word
than talk ourselves to death.
But make no mistake —
this is no theatre of ideas,
only lucid dream.
In here, the passing show
lacks the usual requisite action . . .
but should do in any case.
The anticipation of a long journey
is still possible,
even when there is no horizon.

POUND turns, stops, then turns back to the audience.

You do have lives of your own, you know.
(PAUSE) There's so much to do . . . I . . .
Don't you have homes to go to?
(PAUSE) Well . . . (BEGRUDGINGLY) All right . . .

POUND crosses to his bed. He sits.

The faint sound of a tormented human voice can be heard, howling in another ward. POUND cocks his head. The howling subsides.

POUND: The other day, two women came to visit me. Yes, two. One, who did most of the talking; and one who was so quiet it was like she wasn't here at all. They looked like perfect candidates for the Ez-uversity . . .

BETSY, a university student in her early 20s, enters with a load of books and papers; she carries a portable tape recorder in one hand. She deposits these on POUND'S desk.

BETSY: Mr Pound?

POUND: (LOOKING UP) Hullo!

BETSY: I brought the research.

POUND: Research?

BETSY: From the library . . . at Columbia.

POUND: How did you get in?

BETSY: The, uh, orderly. He . . . he said it would be okay.

POUND: He did?

BETSY: I hope we haven't come at a bad time.

POUND: Who are you?

BETSY: Betsy.

POUND: Betsy?

BETSY: Don't you remember?

POUND: What?

BETSY: Me. Being here before.

POUND: When?

BETSY: Mr Pound!

POUND: What did we talk about?

BETSY: All sorts of things.

POUND: That narrows it down.

BETSY: You were trying to tell me about the Australian Aborigines. You were complaining that the library here at the hospital was no good.

POUND: And the orderly let you in.

BETSY: (NODDING) Mr Brierson.

POUND: And he didn't warn you about me?

BETSY shakes her head.

POUND: C'mere.

BETSY hesitates.

POUND: C'mon, c'mon!

She moves closer.

POUND: What did Brierson say?

BETSY: He said you were feeling depressed. He thought you might not speak to us.

POUND: Yup, that's Brierson. Always splendidly candid about my condition.

BETSY: He wasn't mean about it or anything.

POUND: No, no, of course not. The man's a saint.

BETSY: He said he didn't think you should be here, that you were only confused.

POUND: The guy has no concept of anything at all.

BETSY: He was critical of the Justice Department. He ... he said the State was barbaric.

POUND: Barbaric, eh? Quite a likeable chap, really.

BETSY nods.

BETSY: He said that if you'd just kept quiet you probably wouldn't . . .

POUND: Kept quiet? Nonsense! "The man of understanding can no more sit quiet while his country lets its literature decay than a good doctor could sit quiet while some ignorant child infected itself with tuberculosis . . . under the impression it was merely eating jam tarts."

BETSY: (COMPLIANTLY) It doesn't make any sense, does it?

POUND: What?

BETSY: Calling ourselves modern, and then locking our poets away in insane asylums.

POUND: 'Modern' ended with Hiroshima.

BETSY: But you're a great poet, Mr Pound.

POUND: I'm also a helluva tennis player. So what!

BETSY: It's wrong. What they're doing to you.

POUND: You're not from the Department, are you?

BETSY: No. Margaret and I are from New York. From Columbia University.

POUND: Margaret?

BETSY: (GESTURING) My friend.

POUND looks but sees nothing.

POUND: (ASIDE) And people wonder why I'm paranoid!

BETSY: We caught the Greyhound down from New York last night. Are you sure you don't remember me, Mr Pound?

POUND: Maybe it'll come to me. You're teachers, right?

BETSY: Students. English majors.

BETSY sits on the edge of the desk, letting her legs swing free.

POUND: I see. (BEAT) From New York.

BETSY nods.

POUND: And the orderly let you in.

BETSY: I think he must've felt sorry for us. We'd come such a long way.

POUND: And you didn't have to bribe him?

BETSY: We didn't have anything to bribe him with.

POUND: (LOOKING AT HER) I doubt that.

BETSY glances down at the desk. She reaches out to touch POUND'S typewriter.

POUND: Don't fiddle!

She withdraws her hand.

POUND: Quick reactions . . . I like that!

BETSY: I'm sorry.

POUND: So you should be.

POUND moves to his desk. He covers the typewriter with a towel.

BETSY: Were you working on something?

POUND: Between distractions.

BETSY: If you'd like us to leave . . .

POUND: No! It'll keep. One of the virtues of poetry . . . unlike pate.

POUND picks up a few stray sheets of paper and pegs them to his clothesline.

BETSY: I brought a tape recorder.

POUND: A what?

BETSY: A tape recorder. The last time I was here you said it would be okay if I made some recordings.

POUND: What sort of recordings?

BETSY: Of you.

POUND: I don't think so.

BETSY: You said if I brought you the information you wanted you'd let me record you reading some of your poems.

POUND: Was I awake?

BETSY: Mr Pound!

POUND: Sometimes I nod off in the middle of conversations and people think it means I'm agreeing with em.

BETSY: We had a long discussion about it.

POUND: We did?

BETSY: I'm not making it up.

POUND turns, distracted by a sheet of paper on the floor. He picks it up and examines it.

BETSY: You said you thought it was a good idea.

He pegs the sheet of paper to his clothesline.

BETSY: Mr Pound?

POUND continues looking at the paper he's pegged to the line.

BETSY: Mr Pound.

POUND: Call me "Grampaw".

BETSY: Grampaw?

POUND: All my young visitors call me Grampaw.

BETSY smiles.

POUND: And try being a little less pushy, will you?

(ASIDE) Do I have to direct the thing as well?

POUND and BETSY look into each other's eyes.

POUND: Enchanting.

BETSY: What?

POUND: Your eyes.

BETSY: Thank you.

POUND lingers for a moment, then turns away.

POUND: So . . . you've been travelling all night, huh?

BETSY: Yes. Margaret and I.

POUND: Margaret? (HE LOOKS) Ah yes.

BETSY: She's very shy. Sometimes I even forget she's there, myself. Very self-contained, though.

POUND: Yes. Tremendous self-discipline.

BETSY: She's a very good listener, too.

POUND: I've heard of bit parts, but this is ridiculous.

BETSY: Excuse me?

POUND: Just talking to myself. One of the fringe benefits of being here. Ought to be more careful, eh? They might think I'm mad.

BETSY: I don't think you're mad at all. You just see things a little differently from most people.

POUND: You think so?

BETSY: I'm sure you're just as sane as I am.

POUND glances at the unseen MARGARET then back to BETSY.

POUND: Well, that's a relief. How do *you* feel?

BETSY: A little tired, I guess. But . . .

POUND: No, no. I mean, how do you *feel*? Are you sure you're not from just down the hall?

BETSY: No. From New York.

POUND: Oh . . . good.

BETSY gazes round the room.

BETSY: Gee, there's not much light is there?

POUND: No. They're very particular about the light. They don't want the little there is escaping out the windows so they keep them closed. Think about it. Bureaucracies understand these things. Would you care for a glass of wine?

BETSY: They allow you wine?

POUND: Almost everything! Free country, y'know. What about a sandwich? You look like you could use a sandwich.

POUND bolts to the fridge.

POUND: Lemme see now . . . lemme see . . . what've we got here? Bacon . . . marmalade . . . ketchup. Ah! What about some mayonnaise?

POUND turns, holding up the jar of mayonnaise.

POUND: From Havana!

BETSY: Cuban mayonnaise.

POUND: Hemingway.

POUND takes off the lid and sniffs.

POUND: Totally eclipsed by his prose, I'm afraid; but then it's not easy being a renaissance man these days.

POUND samples some with his finger.

BETSY: A glass of wine would be nice, thank you.

POUND: Wine. Right!

POUND replaces the lid and returns the mayonnaise to the fridge. He crosses to the desk, opens a drawer and rummages through the litter.

POUND: There's a very passable drop of red here somewhere.

He pulls out several bits of paper, some old file cards, a crumpled magazine, a couple of empty jars and a tennis ball. The ball bounces away. Finally, he extracts an already opened bottle of red wine. He holds it up.

POUND: *Chateauneuf de Pape*, 1953. cummings left it when he was here last week. He knows I loathe red.

BETSY: e.e. cummings?

POUND: You know cummings, do you?

POUND uncorks the bottle.

BETSY: He's one of Margaret's favorite poets! He was at Columbia last year reading his poetry, wasn't he Margaret?

POUND glances in the direction of the unseen MARGARET.

POUND: A devotee, eh?

BETSY: She identifies with him.

POUND: Uh-huh.

BETSY: She's read everything he's ever published.

POUND: Extraordinary. One is never very sure where the lovers of verse are these days, and then when you meet one . . . well . . . (BEAT) Is Margaret drinking?

BETSY shakes her head.

POUND: Bad liver?

BETSY: Eczema. She breaks out all over.

POUND: How irritating!

BETSY: Milk has the same effect on her.

POUND looks in Margaret's direction.

POUND: Poor thing! You just can't win, can you?

POUND pours the wine into the two empty jars.

BETSY: You and Mr cummings are good friends, aren't you?

POUND: We've had our spats. Last time I saw him it ended in an argument over some confounded notion of his that he knew the language of bluejays . . . and that man is out on the streets, mind you!

BETSY: Did he mean it?

POUND: Course he meant it! Good poets always mean it. Cantankerous old bastard.

POUND hands a jar of wine to BETSY.

BETSY: Thank you.

POUND: Don't mention it. (LIFTING HIS JAR) Cheers!

BETSY: To your health . . . and long life.

POUND: Why not?!

They drink. POUND obviously doesn't like the taste.

BETSY: (SAVORING THE TASTE) It's good.

POUND: Hmmm.

BETSY has another sip. They sit in silence for a moment.

POUND: So what possessed you to . . .
   [TOGETHER]
BETSY: If someone had told me . . .

   SILENCE.

POUND: Is this the first time . . .
   [TOGETHER]
BETSY: Margaret and I were . . .

POUND: Go ahead.

BETSY: No, you.

POUND: No, I insist.

BETSY: After you.

POUND: What did you say your name was?

BETSY: Betsy.

POUND: Betsy.

BETSY: Short for Elizabeth. It was my grandmother's name. She was from Boston.

POUND: Boston.

BETSY: She worked on the Sacco and Vanzetti Defence Committee.

POUND: Ah.

   POUND finishes his wine in one gulp and pours himself another.

BETSY: My mother says I'm just like her, only she never had an interest in poetry . . . my grandmother, I mean. She was more of a political animal, I guess. You know, a dreamer. Everyone thought she was terribly eccentric.

POUND: Sounds like my father.

BETSY: Was he in politics?

POUND: Politics? No, no, as a matter of fact, he was

an assayer at the Mint, in Philadelphia. Homer. When I was eight he took me down to watch them counting the money. All the silver money in America was counted that year. They didn't miss a nickel. Men stripped to the waist, sweating under the gas flares, shovelling coins into the counting machines. Money was real in those days, y'know. It meant something.

BETSY: We had to borrow fifteen dollars for the bus tickets.

POUND: That's how it starts.

BETSY places her jar on the desk and picks up her handbag.

BETSY: Would you mind if I smoked?

POUND: Are you getting hot?

BETSY looks up.

POUND: Please . . . go ahead. I won't tell.

BETSY extracts a packet of cigarettes from her bag.

BETSY: Do you want one?

POUND: Maybe later.

BETSY shakes a cigarette from her packet.

BETSY: Margaret thinks I smoke too much. She keeps telling me it'll stunt my growth.

POUND: (GLANCING IN MARGARET'S DIRECTION) Yes, well, uh . . . Margaret looks like she'd know about that sort of thing.

POUND lights BETSY's cigarette, then extracts an ashtray from under a pile of manuscripts.

BETSY exhales slowly, then sighs.

BETSY: That's better.

They sit in silence for a moment.

BETSY: So . . . (TAKING ANOTHER PUFF) Can we start the recordings?

POUND: Huh?

BETSY: You know . . . something from *The Cantos* maybe, or . . . well anything you like, really. (BETSY MOVES TO THE TAPE RECORDER) Maybe you could just talk for awhile.

POUND: I thought we'd settled that.

BETSY: But you promised!

POUND: I have no memory of promising any such thing. (BEAT) Why's it so important, anyway?

BETSY: Because what you have to say is worth listening to.

POUND: Nonsense!

BETSY: Because it's a way of making people understand.

POUND: Good Gawd.

BETSY: People will listen.

POUND: Like they did to the radio broadcasts.

BETSY: I'm talking about poetry, Grampaw.

POUND: Part of some English assignment, is it?

BETSY: No.

POUND: Come on!

BETSY: It's not!

POUND: Don't lie to me!

BETSY: I'm not lying!

POUND: Trying to make a name for yerself, are you?

BETSY: No!

POUND: Well what is it, then?

BETSY: You said that a poet should sing the things he cares about.

POUND: Not when it means diverting attention. They might end up thinking I like it here.

BETSY: (ALMOST BEGGING) But it's important!

POUND: "Bird in cage does not sing."

BETSY: If we could just record a few . . .

POUND: Bird in cage   does   not   sing! One finishes saying "cage" between clenched teeth. You notice? The physicality of the word, the way the body imitates the meaning. Bird   in   *cage*   does not sing.

BETSY: (ENTHUSIASTICALLY) I wouldn't even mind getting that.

POUND: Ah, my dear girl, can't you see? The main spring's busted. And nothing can put it right, not until the record's set straight. I have wasted too much time with poetry in here.

BETSY: You've been here so long . . . it would affect anyone.

POUND: But I ain't crazy!

BETSY: I know.

   BEAT.

POUND: You do?

BETSY: I never thought you were crazy to begin with.

POUND: If only I'd studied Confucius earlier, I never would've gotten in to this mess. (BEAT) Maybe I should've stopped the broadcasts after Pearl Harbor.

BETSY: What you said on the radio didn't cause the

deaths of any Americans.

POUND: They still said I was a traitor.

BETSY: You tried to stop the war.

POUND: No. I said too much . . . always too much where it didn't count. They'll never let me forget it either.

BETSY: People make mistakes, Grampaw.

POUND: This was never part of the deal, y'know. I was double-crossed. They were supposed to release me after the insanity hearing. Thirteen years in the bughouse was never part of the agenda.

BETSY: Is that what they said?

POUND: They didn't say a damn thing. It was all nudges and winks. The doctors have been lying for years, telling em I'm incompetent. Ask Overholser. He knows damn well I have my wits about me. Not that he'd ever admit it.

BETSY: They won't be able to keep you here forever. They'll have to release you sometime.

POUND: Not until they've tried me, and they can't try me unless I can prove to em I'm sane.

BETSY: But you're *safe* here!

POUND: Safe. Oh yes! I've been talking myself to sleep for years, deluding myself into believing that the safety of this hell-hole was preferable to taking the bastards on. Well, if I'd been as crazy as they thought I was, I'd be seein things. What was I afraid of? Death? The fear of death is Death.

BETSY: You mustn't let them put you on trial, Grampaw.

POUND: Why not? Why shouldn't I stand up and tell em what I think? You said so yourself — I'm just as sane as you are . . . you and Margaret.

BETSY: They won't let you win. They'll just say you're guilty and execute you. That's how they work. The fact that you're a poet means nothing to them. They don't care about poetry.

POUND: Survival at any cost, eh?

BETSY: You can't do anything if you're dead.

POUND: If a man ain't prepared to take some risks for what he believes in, either his beliefs are no good, or he's no good. So which is it?

BETSY: They'll destroy you.

POUND: No one can hide the truth forever.

POUND turns away. He notices the books and notes BETSY has deposited on his desk.

POUND: What's all this?

BETSY: Oh. Those are the notes you wanted.

POUND: Notes?

BETSY: The information you asked me to bring you.

POUND: What're you talking about?

BETSY: You said you wanted some information about the Australian Aborigines. It was part of our agreement.

POUND: Wait a minute. Wait. I know you. (PROBING) You're supposed to be a Wednesday!

BETSY: A what?

POUND: What day is it today?

BETSY: Saturday.

POUND: That's right. That explains it. We were talking about the Aborigines, right?

BETSY: That's what I've been trying to tell you.

POUND: And you were supposed to come back on a

Wednesday. It was you, wasn't it?

BETSY: I couldn't get away. I had exams.

POUND: (THINKING ALOUD) Or were you a Tuesday?

BETSY: You were asking about the Wandjina. I . . . I brought everything I could find.

POUND: The who?

BETSY: The Wandjina.

POUND: Wandjina.

BETSY: You said it might be a key.

POUND: A key? What sort of key?

BETSY: You said you thought it might have something to do with you being here.

POUND: Wandjina?

BETSY: That's what you said. (BEAT) Maybe if you read through the notes . . .

POUND falls silent.

POUND: Wandjina. Yes. Wandjina. Of course!

BETSY: Grampaw . . .

POUND: I remember one summer walking along an old road and discovering a dead deer. You could feel its presence, weeks, even months, later. I'm sure if I was there now I would still feel it. Then there was that fishing hole full of edible red-fin . . . and that special, shady tree near Sant' Ambrogio — a eucalypt — down the hill from the villa . . . (POUND EXTRACTS SOMETHING FROM HIS POCKET) Here.

He shows BETSY the object in the palm of his hand.

BETSY: What is it?

POUND: A nut. From the tree.

BETSY: Oh.

She reaches out to touch it, but POUND withdraws it into himself. He puts it back in his pocket.

POUND: Places full of power. Sacred places. Places where one feels a contentment, a belonging; where one feels whole.

BETSY: I've always loved the subway. The smell of cigar smoke . . . woollen coats in winter . . . the newsprint. It makes me think of when I was a girl.

POUND: You grew up in the city.

BETSY: New Rochelle.

POUND: Ah!

BETSY: I still love it.

POUND: That's what I'm talking about! Those special, personal places; not special by chance, but because we find parts of ourselves in em, and leave parts of ourselves behind. The parts of the world *we* create. Like the Wandjina.

He crosses to his clothesline filing system.

POUND: A long time ago, some young people — students of Frobenius — came to my house in Rapallo. They had sketches they'd made on one of their expeditions . . . (GRABBING HOLD OF A LARGE PIECE OF PAPER, TURNING IT ROUND TO REVEAL A FULL LENGTH DRAWING OF A WANDJINA FIGURE) Drawings . . . like this one. There are several hundred of them on the walls of caves in the hinterland of Auss'ralia. Look at the expression. It's as if he was sitting squarely on top of his own anxiety.

BETSY: They look sort of like spacemen, don't they?

POUND: Don't be daft! They've got nothing to do with spacemen! If intuition has a face, there it is! And someone has actually drawn it!

BETSY: Without mouths.

POUND: Yes! (PAUSE) So . . . what happened to the mouths?

BETSY: They weren't needed any more.

POUND: Weren't needed?

BETSY: The Aborigines believe the Wandjina created the world, the entire world, with words, with names. All they had to do was name something and it would exist. Trees, mountains, animals. Everything. They say if the Wandjina hadn't been stopped they would've made too many things. So the mouths were taken away.

POUND: Taken away?

BETSY: Removed. To stop the names.

POUND: What do you mean?

BETSY: If they'd kept going, they would've destroyed the world. There would've been too many things.

POUND: (A REVELATION) So it was a punishment!

BETSY: I think you better read the notes.

POUND: I knew it! If only I hadn't been so dumb.

BETSY: What're you talking about, Grampaw?

POUND: The tribe that made these . . .
    (POINTING TO THE DRAWING)
    had sixteen words for water!
    Nomad, the antithesis of noman,
    knows the sacred places.
    Is fluid and capable of exactitude,
    without writing, without books or libraries,
    without credit or stock markets,

        precisely because he is in his place.
        The Land is alive.
        It has everything to do with his life!
        Sixteen words for water!
        (PAUSE)
        How many do you have?

BETSY: (SHRUGS) Water.

POUND: Precisely! A vain abstraction, aided by adjectives.

BETSY: Why does it matter?

POUND: Because rain water is different from surface water,
    and salt water is not the same as fresh.
    It has to do with immediacy —
    a knowledge of the world at first-hand.
    "Periplum, not as land looks on a map
    but as sea bord seen by men sailing."
    Otherwise . . . we look at life
    as through a two-way mirror.

BETSY: Sixteen words for water.

POUND: So how is it that the Aborigines had such ideas about the world and never wrote a book, or built a chapel, or composed a fugue, or invented an atom bomb?

BETSY: Maybe they had no need for them.

POUND: Because they *know* who they are! "Our humanity is counterfeit; our liberty, cankered with simulation." Wrong from the start.

BETSY: You can say too much sometimes, Grampaw. Sometimes you have to stop talking so that people can hear what you've said.

POUND: Only when one is finished with creation. The difference between the Wandjina and me is that it was the gods who took their mouths away . . .

mine was removed by the State.

BETSY: Sometimes silence can be more powerful than words.

POUND: Those without confidence in banksia
and spinifex for lack of education
must have thought Terra Australis a lost
    land —
an aberrant continent —
where everything is back to front.
Even now, the whitemen wander
uncertain, uncomfortable;
and not for want of plumbing or electricity,
but because they do not understand where
    they are.
I am talking about the power of the Land.
'No one prospers unless everyone prospers'
was the bushman's law;
vis a vis: the whiteman's grace sez:
'if I can't have it, you won't either'.
The stance of men who are threatened —
unable to embrace the Land — in the
    European
produces self-deprecation; produces war
whose language is barricade,
wishing fauns cavorted on sand dunes,
dreaming of genii riding kangaroo.
We speak with a thousand borrowed voices
calling them our own, and wonder
why we cannot trust ourselves.
We define ourselves by what we are not.

BETSY pauses for a moment, reflecting on what he has said.

BETSY: You are not an Aborigine, Grampaw. You are a poet . . . and a very great poet.

POUND: Yes, Ouan Jin! The man of letters. The man

with an education. "A man on whom the sun has gone down." (PAUSE) But I am also related to them! (POINTING) To the Wandjina! And so are you!

BETSY: We are no longer tribal people.

POUND: We are all tribal people under the skin.
And we deny this at the expense
of tearing ourselves in half . . .
which we do every day, very well —
the tearing, I mean. We have made it in to an art . . .
Some in the name of competitiveness,
some from a fear of scarcity,
some believing Nature is the enemy.
But the Dreaming lives in each of us —
the tides of kinship and a susceptibility
for seeing ourselves in the Land
when we stop and look.
"The gods have never left us."

BETSY: There are lots of different kinds of worlds. You can't live in all of them.

POUND: The trick is to live even in one!

BETSY: The trick is to stay alive.

POUND: At what cost?

BETSY and POUND regard each other in silence.

BETSY: You scare me, Grampaw.

POUND: That's because you see me as a metaphor. But there is wisdom in recognising that a desk is a desk and a chair, a chair. We are not so terribly different from the Aborigines, you know . . . except our language does not make us custodians of the Earth, but Earth's adversaries. A man cannot live in fragments. He must know the place he started from and then let others know.

BETSY: They'll call it treason.

POUND: They can call it whatever they like. But the worst treason is the one we commit against ourselves — speaking when we should be silent; or worse, being silent when we should speak.

BETSY: And if they kill you?

POUND: So long as the money-lenders sleep peacefully in their beds there will be no end to war. Two world wars in one century and more to come, arranged by men with blank eyes, setting corpses to banquet at the behest of usury. And who pays for their greed? Us. Always. With our lives. And still we go on voting the asses in who pass the laws and make the deals so the bankers won't go begging. "Love of money beyond all other love, gain at the expense of everything that is admirable." Those who can still see and speak must make themselves heard.

A PAUSE.

BETSY: That sounds like Communism.

POUND: Communism?!

BETSY: If they hear you talk like that . . .

POUND: Communism hain't even practised by the higher mammals! Wake up, girl! Wild dogs collaborate! I wouldn't be caught dead with Communism. Compared to me, Eisenhower's practically a fellow traveller.

A PAUSE. POUND, thinking better of his outburst.

POUND: Sorry.

BETSY: You're going to let them try you, aren't you?

POUND: I'm going to say what I have to say.

BETSY: It won't bring you any peace.

POUND: Peace comes of good manners, and manners are from the earth and water and the knowledge that comes of being where one belongs. I have lost contact with the Earth.

BETSY: I shouldn't have come.

POUND draws closer.

POUND: You came here to save me, didn't you?

BETSY: I tried.

POUND: You mad at me?

BETSY: I love you.

SILENCE. Before POUND has a chance to speak, the door opens and the WOMAN from the Department of Justice enters. POUND and BETSY turn.

WOMAN: Oh, I'm sorry. They didn't tell me you had a visitor.

POUND: Well, well, well . . . the Department of Justice! (HE RAISES HIS ARM IN GREETING, STOPPING SHORT OF A FASCIST SALUTE. THEY SHAKE HANDS.) How are you, my dear?

WOMAN: Mr Pound.

POUND: The pleasure is all mine. And let me introduce you to . . .

WOMAN: Hello Betsy.

BETSY: (SHEEPISHLY) Hello.

WOMAN: Margaret.

POUND blinks in surprise, his glance moving between the WOMAN and the unseen MARGARET.

POUND: You know each other?

WOMAN: Only professionally.

POUND turns to BETSY.

BETSY: It's not like you think, Grampaw.

POUND: What?

BETSY: I had to see you.

WOMAN: (TO BETSY) So how did it go?

BETSY: I don't want to talk about it.

POUND: Talk about what?

WOMAN: (TO BETSY) Did he tell you about Australia?

BETSY: Not now, please.

POUND: What is this?

BETSY: I can explain everything.

POUND: Did she send you?

BETSY: No. It's not like that at all.

POUND: Would someone mind telling me what's going on?

WOMAN: Betsy's been sending us petitions for the past twelve months, trying to have you pardoned.

BETSY: She told me to stay away.

WOMAN: She thinks if I tell them you're sane the government will execute you.

BETSY: Don't trust her, Grampaw.

WOMAN: She thinks you've been victimised.

BETSY: It's true!

WOMAN: She identifies with you.

POUND: How do you know each other?

BETSY: (TO WOMAN) Don't.

WOMAN: Betsy's one of my patients.

BETSY: You're the one who needs a shrink.

WOMAN: Her mother and I are old friends.

BETSY: Leave her out of it!

WOMAN: I'm sorry if she's disturbed you, Mr Pound.

POUND: Not at all.

BETSY: I can explain everything, Grampaw.

POUND: You don't have to.

BETSY: But I want you to know how I feel.

POUND: It's all right. (AFFECTIONATELY) You've already told me.

WOMAN: What's going on?

POUND: Oh, you would've had to have been here, my dear. Betsy and I . . . and, uh, Margaret, have had a very interesting talk. Haven't we?

WOMAN: I see.

POUND: You do?

WOMAN: (TO BETSY) Did you get what you wanted?

BETSY: I'm not talking to you.

WOMAN: (TO BETSY) Maybe you better run along, now.

BETSY: Grampaw!

POUND: She's my guest.

A PAUSE.

WOMAN: I'm afraid I have some bad news for you, Mr Pound. I thought I'd better come myself.

POUND: (TO BETSY) Notice how she prolongs the suspense for dramatic effect.

WOMAN: It's not what you think.

POUND: You told them I was sane, didn't you?

WOMAN: Yes, I did.

POUND: Good!

WOMAN: I also told them I believed you'd been using insanity as a way of escaping the charges.

POUND: Excellent tactic!

WOMAN: As far as I'm concerned there's no reason at all why you shouldn't be put on trial.

POUND: Now you're talking!

BETSY: Why can't you just leave him alone?

WOMAN: I'm sorry, Mr Pound.

POUND: Oh, don't be sorry, my dear. I'm looking forward to it.

BETSY: Haven't you hurt him enough?

WOMAN: You can put your tape recorder away, Betsy. You've won.

POUND: What?

BETSY: (To WOMAN) Don't tell him! You have no right!

WOMAN: She believed it was a way of protecting you.

POUND: Protecting me?

WOMAN: She thought if she could get you on tape . . .

BETSY: (To WOMAN) No! Please.

WOMAN: But he's not crazy, Betsy.

POUND turns to BETSY.

BETSY: I didn't want them to hurt you, Grampaw.

POUND: Yes . . . I know. (A LONG PAUSE . . . THEN HE TURNS TO THE WOMAN) What do you mean, she won?

WOMAN: I mean, they wouldn't listen to me.

POUND: What're you talking about?

WOMAN: Doctor Overholser still seems to think you're suffering from some kind of psychotic disorder. I'm afraid the panel's accepted his recommendation. They've decided you're unfit to enter a plea.

POUND: Unfit!

WOMAN: Incapable.

POUND: On what grounds?

WOMAN: Doctor Overholser doesn't believe you're mentally competent.

BETSY: You mean they're not going to try him?

POUND: She means they're a pack of cowards.

WOMAN: I did what I could, Mr Pound.

BETSY: He never should've been arrested in the first place.

WOMAN: Stay out of this!

POUND: Good strategy, my dear, keeping Pound away from the forum of a courtroom.

BETSY: (TO POUND) But that means they can't touch you.

WOMAN: It's finished.

POUND: Like hell it is!

BETSY: Don't argue with her.

POUND: They don't know what they're talking about!

BETSY: Leave it, Grampaw.

POUND: They haven't proven a damn thing!

WOMAN: They don't have to.

A PAUSE.

POUND: They can't keep me locked up here forever.

WOMAN: No.

POUND: So what're they gonna do? Hang me without a trial?

WOMAN: I know you're sane, believe me. And I would've much rather seen you answer the charge of treason, even *with* the death penalty. At least it would've been settled.

POUND: What're you driving at?

WOMAN: They're going to release you.

POUND: Release me?
[TOGETHER]

BETSY: What!

WOMAN: You've been judged incurably insane. They've decided you'll never be able to stand trial. You're to be placed in the care of your wife. It's over, Mr Pound.

BETSY: You mean he doesn't have to stay here any more?

POUND: (TO WOMAN) They didn't believe you.

WOMAN: They already had their minds made up. (TO POUND) You were right . . . my report was only a formality. It would seem that what I think and say no longer counts.

BETSY: You're free, Grampaw!

POUND looks at BETSY, then turns to the WOMAN.

POUND: (PROFOUNDLY) No!

POUND, suddenly shattered, moves to his bed and sits down. BETSY looks at him, then at the WOMAN.

BETSY: But they're going to let him go. He's safe now.

WOMAN: Yes. (BEAT) Safe.

The WOMAN crosses to POUND.

WOMAN: I wanted you to know . . . I'm leaving the Department. I had to go against what I believed in to tell the truth about you. I don't think I could've lived with myself if I hadn't. You were right. They didn't take me seriously. They threw it in my face. Sometimes to protect yourself you have to walk away. It's a different world out there, Mr Pound. Being louder and angrier won't make them listen any more. I'm sorry.

The WOMAN turns to BETSY. They regard one another in silence.

WOMAN: (TO BOTH POUND AND BETSY) Goodbye.

The WOMAN exits.

POUND: All my enemies have turned to dust.

BETSY: What does it mean?

POUND: It means that nothing, nothing will be rectified.

The STAGE LIGHTS DIM. A SPOT comes on over POUND. He stands. The SILENCE is broken by howling — the sounds of a tormented human being somewhere OFF-STAGE. POUND cocks his head, listening.

POUND: You see? Drammer* is reduced to this.
The man gave everything he had.
An unconfident country will take it all,
give nothing in return . . .
then you awake, wordless, with the moon in
 the window.
(PAUSE)

* drama

One belongs to the world, or to nothing.

STAGE LIGHTS SLOWLY UP. POUND sits down on the bed. BETSY holds the microphone out toward him.

BETSY: Thank you for doing this for us.

POUND: It may be the last thing I do. Silence is beginning to look more and more appealing. I suppose one can be captured by it.

She twists the knob on the tape recorder and moves the mike closer to his mouth.

POUND: Great skill precedes creation.
    The knowledge of plants and birds
    serves better than a stipend;
    A direct feeling.
    "Manners are from the earth and from water;
    they arise out of hills and streams."
    The Land, an extension of the body.
    There are still those who walk the Earth
    and know this, who are attuned to
    the distribution of the spirits of children.
    And those who come from other places,
    for whom custom is only business,
    have no ears for the stories the Earth can tell —
    and no knowledge . . .
    More isolated than I, in my hell-hole,
    dreaming of the Wandjina . . .

LIGHTS OUT.

THE END